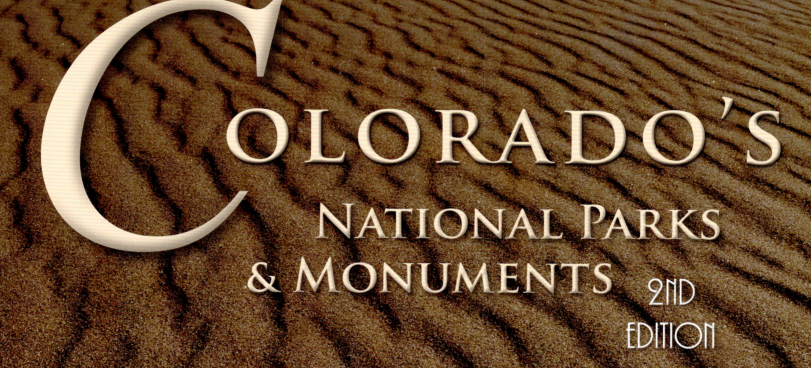

Colorado's
National Parks
& Monuments 2nd Edition

Photography and Essays by

Grant Collier

Collier Publishing LLC
Arvada, CO

ISBN # 978-1-935694-51-9

Published by Collier Publishing LLC
https://www.collierpublishing.com

Cover Photo: Longs Peak rises high above Bear Lake in Rocky Mountain National Park.
Inside Flap Photo: A juniper tree frames spectacular scenery in Colorado National Monument.
Author photo taken by José Low.

Back Cover Photos:
Top Left: The full moon sets over Longs Peak in Rocky Mountain National Park.
Top Right: The Sangre de Cristo Mountains rise above immense mounds of sand in the Great Sand Dunes.
Bottom Left: Painted Wall View in Black Canyon offers a dramatic view of the Gunnison River.
Bottom Right: Spruce Tree House is the third largest cliff dwelling in Mesa Verde National Park.

Acknowledgments

I would like to thank Rex Mumford and his two assistants for guiding me down the Green River in Dinosaur National Monument and the guides at Dinosaur Expeditions for leading me down the Yampa River in Dinosaur National Monument. I would also like to thank Amy Stogner, who proofread the text and Elizabeth Greco, Kay Homer, and Alicia Hewlett, who provided assistance on the design of the book. Thanks to Nat Coalson, who offered technical advice on the cover design and to Erik Stensland, who told me about a few lesser-known places to photograph in Rocky Mountain National Park.

References

http://igp.colorado.edu/
https://obamawhitehouse.archives.gov
https://www.blm.gov/
http://www.chimneyrockco.org/
https://www.fs.fed.us/
https://www.nps.gov/
Burns, Ken; *The National Parks: America's Best Idea.* Public Broadcasting Service (PBS), 2009.
Halka, Chronic; Williams Felicie, *Roadside Geology of Colorado.* Missoula, Montana: Mountain Press Publishing Company, 2002.
Hagood, Allen; West, Linda, *Dinosaur: The Story Behind the Scenery.* KC Publications, Inc., 1999.
Kania, Alan J., *Images of America, Colorado National Monument.* Charleston, SC: Arcadia Publishing, 2008.
Sutton, Carolyn, *The Family Guide to Colorado's National Parks and Monuments.* Englewood, CO: Westcliffe Publishers, 2006.

Colorado Map

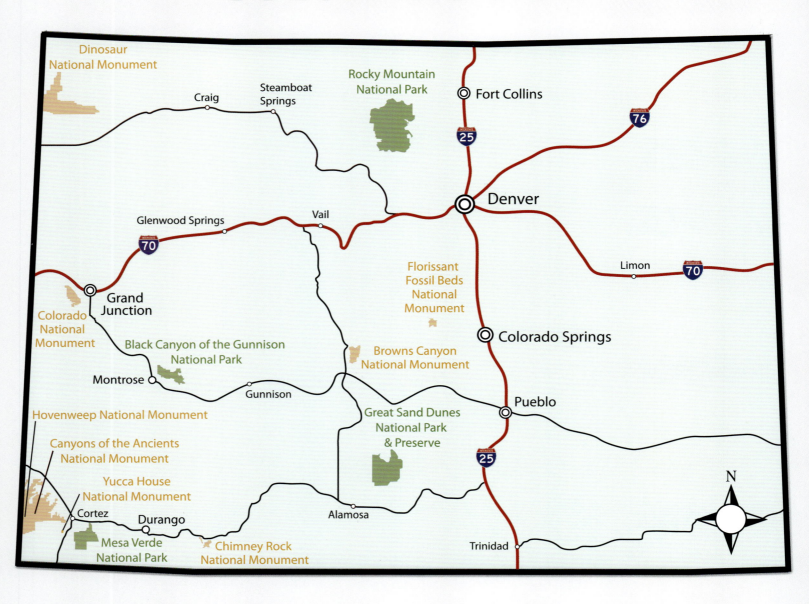

CONTENTS

NATIONAL PARKS

Rocky Mountain
National Park
p. 9

Great Sand Dunes
National Park & Preserve
p. 37

Black Canyon
of the Gunnison
National Park
p. 61

Mesa Verde
National Park
p. 81

NATIONAL MONUMENTS

Dinosaur
National Monument
p. 105

Colorado
National Monument
p. 125

Canyons of the Ancients
National Monument
p. 143

Hovenweep
National Monument
p. 161

Yucca House
National Monument
p. 169

Chimney Rock
National Monument
p. 175

Browns Canyon
National Monument
p. 181

Florissant Fossil Beds
National Monument
p. 187

INTRODUCTION

On an overcast summer day, I turn off a highway onto a small dirt road that leads toward a barren landscape of pinyon pines and junipers. I don't see any fresh tracks on the road and know that this area has probably not been visited since the downpour two days ago. It is the middle of the summer monsoon season, and I realize that it could rain again today. However, I am determined to find a remote Ancestral Puebloan ruin that is tucked away somewhere in this vast landscape.

I reach the end of the road and set out on foot along a trail marked only by an occasional rock cairn. After a relatively short hike, I spot the ruin I have come to photograph. This dwelling was built 1,000 years ago by Ancestral Puebloans, who inhabited the Four Corners area and built remarkable stone mason structures throughout the region.

As I approach the ruin, I hear a loud crack of thunder and sheets of rain begin falling from the heavens, soaking my clothes and camera bag. I quickly head under a rock alcove that is surrounded by an ancient, crumbling stone wall. The rain is now coming down even harder, and lightning bolts crash all around me, but the alcove is perfectly protected from the elements.

Huddled beneath the rocks and looking out into the desolate landscape, I begin to feel a greater appreciation for the Native Americans. For a brief moment, I am transported back in time. I am using this ruin for shelter and protection, just like they did one thousand years ago. I realize how well adapted their structures were for the unpredictable weather along the Colorado Plateau.

As the storm stretches on, I begin to wonder if I will have to spend the night in this alcove. My car is less than a mile away, but I have not brought a flashlight and don't want to wander back in this intense thunderstorm. I become cold, tired, hungry, and inexplicably happy. It is rare in life that we can return to our roots in nature and live in the moment, without cell phones, computers, or other distractions. At times like this, we are forced to focus only on our immediate surroundings and can admire both the beauty and power of nature.

I realize that I may not have had this brief but transcendent moment if not for the vision and tireless work of those who came before me. When Lewis and Clark journeyed across the American West on their historic expedition to the Pacific Ocean, they encountered a rugged, primitive, and unimaginably beautiful landscape. The Native Americans who had lived in this wilderness for over 10,000 years had altered the environment to some extent, but it remained, at its core, a wild and untamed territory.

In the years following the Lewis and Clark expedition, American settlers drastically altered the landscape of the West. They logged virgin forests, mined for gold, silver, and coal, and killed countless wild animals. By the end of the 19th century, the tremendous herds of bison that once roamed the Great Plains had been driven to the brink of extinction. Populations of smaller mammals, including beavers and otters, also dropped precipitously. This was all done in the name of progress and Manifest Destiny.

Fortunately, there were men who realized the intrinsic value of raw, unspoiled wilderness. In 1872, F.V. Hayden's report on the Wyoming territory convinced the United States Congress to establish Yellowstone National Park. This was the first national park in the world, and it was the first time a government set aside vast acres of land for the good of all of its citizens.

The national parks were called "the best idea we ever had" by Wallace Stegner, but this idea was slow to take shape, as the parks were initially underfunded and mismanaged. However, legendary men like John Muir, Theodore Roosevelt, and Stephen Mather helped transform the parks from an archaic system into the one that we know today.

Unfortunately, even now, the park system has its flaws. With ever-increasing numbers of visitors, some of the parks have traffic backed up for miles and throngs of people that give the land the feeling of a theme park rather than a wilderness area. However, even in the most visited parks, one can, with a little effort, still find endless acres of unfathomably beautiful, primordial scenery that embodies the essence of the American West.

Encouragingly, the park system has taken a different approach to the management of some of the newer national monuments. The main attractions in these monuments are not widely publicized, and visitors are left to discover them on their own. This is the case with Canyons of the Ancients National Monument, where I now sit waiting out the storm. Although the monument has a large visitor center, the rangers remain secretive about the location of most of the ruins. I have had to find them on my own, using the knowledge I have gained during twenty-five years of exploring the Colorado wilderness. I often find myself completely alone in a landscape that has changed little since the Ancestral Puebloans lived here one thousand years ago.

As the hours roll by and my eyes grow weary of looking out onto the rain-soaked landscape, I find a flat spot inside the alcove and lie down to rest and possibly sleep. However, as the sun begins to set over the horizon, the rain finally subsides. I know I'll have at least forty minutes of twilight to illuminate the path back, and I quickly head toward my car. For the moment, I am happy to be returning to civilization and am looking forward to a warm meal. But I also feel a tinge of regret that I won't be spending a cold, rainy night in a mystical ruin built long before white men ever set foot on this land.

Rocky Mountain National Park contains immense mountain peaks rising abruptly from the flat landscape of the Great Plains. The centerpiece of the park is 14,000-foot Longs Peak, which served as a landmark to early pioneers and attracts thousands of mountain climbers today.

Although the massive mountains that make up the park may seem changeless and immutable, they have existed for only a fraction of Earth's history. Just 70 million years ago, Colorado was a low-lying landscape that had been periodically covered by shallow seas. Around this time, the Pacific and North American continental plates collided, pushing

Rocky Mountain National Park

the land upward and forming the Rocky Mountains. This period of mountain building was known as the Laramie Orogeny and lasted for approximately 30 million years.

Following this uplift, tremendous amounts of magma squeezed through cracks in the earth's surface, forming a series of volcanoes stretching from the Front Range to the San Juan Mountains. Remnants of this volcanic activity can be found throughout Rocky Mountain National Park, and an ancient volcano called Specimen Mountain still exists inside the park.

The Rockies were beset not only by fire but also by ice. Beginning approximately 2.6 million years ago, Earth was besieged by an ice age that caused enormous glaciers to periodically advance and retreat into Colorado. These glaciers carved out some of the more spectacular scenery in Rocky Mountain National Park, including steep valleys, moraines, tarns, and cirques. One particularly massive glacier created Moraine Park and formed the 9000-foot-tall Eagle Cliff Mountain.

Following the retreat of the last glaciers around 12,500 years ago, the climate became more suitable for human habitation in Colorado's mountains. The first humans entered what is now Rocky Mountain National Park around 12,000 years ago. Evidence suggests that the Clovis, Archaic, and Ceramic cultures all inhabited the park.

Around 1300 A.D., the Ute Indians came to Colorado and began hunting in Rocky Mountain National Park during summer. They were joined in the area by the Arapaho Indians in the late 1700s. However, following the arrival of American settlers in 1859, these Native Americans were driven onto reservations outside of the state.

In 1820, Stephen H. Long led the first United States expedition to explore the area around Rocky Mountain National Park. Although Longs Peak now permanently bears his name, Stephen and his men did not attempt to climb this mountain. This feat was first accomplished by a group of men that included John Wesley Powell and William N. Byers in 1868.

The first white settler in Estes Park was Joel Estes, who arrived in 1860. Estes lived in the valley for only six years, after which he sold his land to Griffith Evans, who established a dude ranch on the property. One of the guests at Evans' ranch was an Englishman known as the Earl of Dunraven. Dunraven was captivated by the pristine landscape, and he used dubious methods in an attempt to acquire vast acres of land as his own private game reserve. Several of the early residents fiercely opposed this land grab, and the Earl ultimately ended up with around 8,000 acres.

Another early resident of Estes Park was a writer and naturalist named Enos A. Mills. Unlike the Earl of Dunraven, Mills wanted to preserve the spectacular mountains above Estes Park as public lands accessible to all Americans. He spent many years lobbying to establish a national park, and in 1915 President Woodrow Wilson signed a bill creating Rocky Mountain National Park.

Although a superintendent was appointed for the park, he had a limited budget, and the government was only able to provide basic facilities. Much of the early development was done by landowners, who were able to keep private property they owned within the park prior to 1915. These men constructed lodges to host visitors, and they also built and maintained roads and trails around the park.

As visitation to Rocky Mountain National Park

increased after World War I, the patchwork array of facilities and trails was deemed inadequate, and the government was given more money to accommodate tourists.

In September of 1929, construction began on Trail Ridge Road. This road was built to replace Fall River Road, which was too narrow and offered limited scenic overlooks. The new road reached Grand Lake on the other side of the Continental Divide in 1938. It has a maximum elevation of 12,183 feet, making it the highest paved through road in the United States.

During the Great Depression of the 1930s, many other projects were completed within the park. The Civilian Conservation Corps built trails and buildings, planted trees, and put out wildfires.

The number of visitors to the national park declined significantly during World War II, and many of the facilities fell into disrepair. When visitation increased following the war, Congress approved the Mission 66 program, which aimed to dramatically improve visitor services by 1966. Three new visitor centers were constructed, and several new campgrounds and parking lots were built.

As visitation continued to increase throughout the 1960s and 1970s, the park service became more concerned about the impact of tourism on the environment. Rangers began assigning backcountry permits, and shuttle buses were introduced to reduce the impact of automobiles.

The protection and management of wildlife in the park also became a priority. Early in the park's history, predators such as wolves, black bears, and mountain lions were killed to accommodate visitors. With the predators gone, populations of prey animals, including mule deer and elk, rose dramatically. Overgrazing by elk, who gnaw on the bark of trees, destroyed stands of willow and aspen throughout the park. As a result, the National Park Service began building fences around large stands of trees and is now permitted to cull some of the elk population.

Another environmental issue was the pine beetle infestations, which hit the west side of the park especially hard during droughts in the early 2000s. The dead trees left behind by these infestations can burn longer and more easily during a forest fire than living trees. This exacerbated the Cameron Peak and East Troublesome wildfires in 2020. These were the two largest fires in Colorado's recorded history, and they burned vast swaths of land in and around Rocky Mountain National Park.

Although fires are often a natural occurrence that can help restore balance in nature, recent fires have been far more severe due to forest mismanagement and climate change.

Nature has a remarkable ability to recover, and forests can regrow. However, they have more difficulty recovering after large, high-intensity fires. Drought and higher temperatures from climate change can make this even more challenging. If climate change continues unabated, nature's ability to rebuild and adapt will be pushed to the limit. Millions of animal and plant species across the planet could become extinct and entire ecosystems could collapse.

Today, setting aside land as national parks and wilderness areas is not enough to completely protect these environments. Everything on Earth is irrevocably intertwined. Outside forces like climate change can be just as devastating to natural areas as internal forces. To truly protect any part of our planet, we must protect all of it.

Above: A waterfall flows beneath Dragon's Tail near Emerald Lake.
p. 8: Three bull elk rest beneath spectacular mountain scenery on a summer afternoon.

Longs Peak is seen through Rock Cut along Trail Ridge Road.

Flowers sprout from lily pads on Nymph Lake in July.

Paintbrush grows alongside a sapling on the west side of the park.

A small waterfall flows through a forest along Fall River Road.

The moon sets over Longs Peak as the first light of day illuminates the mountain.

Numerous meteors streak above Longs Peak during the Geminids Meteor Shower in December.

A large meteor burns up in the atmosphere above Lily Lake during the Geminids shower.

Aspen trees that have been gnawed on by elk stand near the Fern Lake Trailhead.

Boulder Brook flows through an aspen forest during the height of fall color.

The gnarled branches of a fallen tree lie in Moraine Park after a snowstorm.

A mixture of living and deceased trees stand along Fall River Road.

Snow-covered aspen and pine trees grow along Bear Lake Road.

Pines trees are covered with large amounts of snow along Trail Ridge Road.

The sun peeks through the clouds following a large snowstorm in Moraine Park.

Early morning light illuminates Hallett Peak, which is reflected in Dream Lake.

Remarkable patterns have formed in the bark of trees in Horseshoe Park.

Comet NEOWISE sets behind rock crags on Lily Mountain on a summer night.

Wildflowers grow beneath Hallett Peak, which is lit by the rising sun.

Dramatic alpine scenery is reflected in Sprague Lake on a summer morning.

Star trails from a two-hour exposure streak above the gnarled branches of a dead tree.

The Big Dipper is seen above Chapin, Chiquita, and Ypsilon Mountains.

The moon rises above Deer Mountain during twilight.

A lone elk stands atop barren alpine scenery along Trail Ridge Road.

Colorful aspen and pine trees stand on a hillside after an autumn snowstorm.

Lodgepole pines are reflected in Sprague Lake on a summer morning.

Orange and yellow aspen trees frame Bear Lake and 14,000-foot Longs Peak.

Intricate patterns formed in the ice in Dream Lake during the depths of winter.

Aspen trees have grown in remarkable, curvy shapes near Bear Lake Road.

Great Sand Dunes National Park and Preserve in southern Colorado contains enormous knolls of sand that rise high above the San Luis Valley. These dunes twist and undulate along the base of the Sangre de Cristo Mountains, giving them, as Zebulon Pike wrote, the appearance "of a sea in storm." Fierce winds constantly reshape the highest sand deposits, carving mesmerizing patterns throughout the landscape.

For nearly two centuries, geologists have been trying to understand how such an immense amount of sand got deposited here. They currently believe that an enormous lake, called Lake

GREAT SAND DUNES
NATIONAL PARK & PRESERVE

Alamosa, covered much of the San Luis Valley from 3 million years ago until 440,000 years ago. This lake, along with some smaller lakes that succeeded it, left behind a giant sheet of sand in the valley.

Winds in the San Luis Valley generally blow in a northeasterly direction, carrying sand toward the Sangre de Cristo Mountains. During storms, the wind blows down mountain passes in the opposite direction, forcing the sand to pile up higher and higher at the base of the mountains. Medano Creek and Sand Creek also carry sand down from the mountain passes back onto the valley floor, where some of it is eventually deposited back onto the dunes.

The persistent winds and huge supply of sand has caused the Great Sand Dunes to rise 750 feet above the valley floor, making them the tallest sand dunes in North America. The dunes cover 30 square miles and contain an estimated 4.8 billion cubic meters of sand. A vast amount of sand still exists in the sand sheet left by Lake Alamosa, so it's possible the dunes could grow even higher.

The first humans to lay eyes on the Great Sand Dunes were probably the Clovis people, who arrived in the area around 11,000 years ago. There is evidence that these Native Americans hunted mammoths at a site near the dunes. Spear points from both the Clovis culture and their descendants, the Folsom people, have been found throughout the San Luis Valley.

From 1300 A.D. to 1900 A.D., the region was inhabited by the Navajos, Utes, Jicarilla Apaches, and Pueblo Indians. These Native Americans hunted wild game and used bark from trees in the dunes for food and medicine.

Two of the earliest European explorers to enter the San Luis Valley were Don Diego de Vargas in 1694 and Juan Bautista de Anza in 1776. Both of these men were Spanish territorial governors, and they provided accounts of the valley, though neither mentioned the Great Sand Dunes.

American explorer Zebulon Pike made the first written account of the dunes during his expedition to the West in 1807. Pike wrote: "After marching some miles, we discovered…at the foot of the White Mountains [today's Sangre de Cristo Mountains] which we were then descending, sandy hills…The Sand-hills extended up and down the foot of the White Mountains about 15 miles, and appeared to be about 5 miles in width."

Following Pike's expedition, many fur traders and trappers came to the San Luis Valley in search of valuable beaver pelts. Also, in the mid-1800s, John Fremont and Captain John Gunnison led separate expeditions that passed alongside the dunes in search of railroad routes to the Pacific Ocean. Although the transcontinental railroad was not built in this region, these explorers helped open the San Luis Valley for settlement.

The early homesteaders in the valley lived in fear of the Native Americans, who resisted the intrusion of the white settlers on their homeland. In 1858, Fort Garland was established twenty miles southeast of the dunes to afford the settlers some protection.

Among the early residents were Ulysses Herard and his family, who established a ranch in 1875 along what is now the Medano Pass Primitive Road in Great Sand Dunes National Preserve. The Herards raised horses and cattle and built a fish hatchery and a post office on their property. Other settlers who established homesteads near the sand dunes were Teofilo Trujillo and his family, who raised sheep, and Frank and Virginia Wellington, who built a cabin near the present-day campground.

In the 1920s, the sand dunes became threatened by companies that considered mining the sand for gold or using it to make concrete. The Volcanic Mining Company established a gold mill on the dunes in 1932, but so little gold was recovered that the operation was quickly abandoned.

In order to ensure that the dunes would not be damaged by commercial development, the Monte Vista chapter of the Philanthropic and Educational Organization for Women began campaigning for the protection of the land in 1932. Their goal was realized that same year when Herbert Hoover signed a bill designating the Great Sand Dunes as a national monument.

The dunes gained further protection in October of 1976 when they were designated a National Wilderness Area. In the first years of the 21st century, the government acquired additional territory around the dunes, and the land became a national park and preserve in September of 2004.

The Great Sand Dunes were designated a national park not only because of the spectacular hills of sand but also because of the enormous ecological diversity around the dunes. The park and preserve encompass seven distinct ecosystems, which provide habitat for a multitude of wildlife.

The only ecosystem that does not support much animal life is the dunefield itself. A coyote may occasionally wander onto it, but the kangaroo rat is the only mammal that can live in this harsh environment.

The landscape is more habitable on the sand sheets at the base of the dunes. Pronghorn antelope can often be seen here, and over 2,000 bison currently roam on lands owned by the Nature Conservancy inside the park.

Closer to the mountains, the sandy environment gives way to a pinyon-juniper woodland. Mule deer, cottontail rabbits, mountain lions, bobcats, and great horned owls can all be found here. At higher elevations, pine trees and aspen trees thrive. Black bears, northern goshawks, and brown bats all inhabit this montane forest.

The forest gradually gives way to less-forgiving sub-alpine and then alpine terrain. This region has rugged mountains rising over 13,000 feet, including Herard Peak, Cleveland Peak, and Tijeras Peak. It is home to marmots and ptarmigans and is a seasonal home to birds like the horned lark.

The remarkable array of wildlife and ecosystems within the Great Sand Dunes combine to form a landscape like no other in Colorado. With its status as a national park and preserve, we can be assured that people will enjoy this landscape long into the future. Like the Native Americans thousands of years ago, future generations will be able to feel the timeless pulse of life as bison roam the plains beneath enormous dunes and craggy peaks.

Above: Sinuous patterns have formed along the eastern edge of the dunes.
p. 36: Relentless winds have sculpted mesmerizing patterns into the dunes.

This snow-covered Sangre de Cristo Mountains loom above the Great Sand Dunes.

Cottonwood trees are silhouetted against the base of the dunes.

Late evening light illuminates numerous ripples in the dunes.

Crestone Peak and Crestone Needle rise high above the Great Sand Dunes.

A bolt of lightning strikes the dunes during an intense thunderstorm.

Mount Herard is visible above immense mounds of sand at the top of the dunes.

Medano Creek comes to an abrupt end as the water is absorbed by sand.

Wildflowers and fall colors bring the park alive with color in late September.

Verdant plant life grows near Medano Creek on the eastern side of the dunes.

Mount Zwischen rises above sand sheets at the base of the dunes.

Intricate patterns can be found etched in the sand throughout the dunes.

The evening sun creates a dramatic interplay of light and shadow on the dunes.

Clouds float above the Sangre de Cristo Mountains following an early winter snowstorm.

Prairie grasses grow beneath the highest dune in the park, called Star Dune.

Walls of sand rise above a cottonwood tree in autumn.

Sunflowers grow in improbable places high atop the dunes.

Dramatic light illuminates Carbonate Mountain, located southeast of the dunes.

A colorful sunset lights up the sky above Medano Creek during spring runoff.

Black Canyon of the Gunnison National Park in western Colorado is one of the most inhospitable places in the state. From the rim, the canyon plunges almost straight down into a colossal abyss. Far below, the river looks like a tiny ribbon of water. However, those who have dared travel through the canyon know that the river rages with immense power as it winds through the rocky terrain. Many sections of the river are designated "unraftable," and even today, only a small number of hardy souls have made a complete river passage through the canyon.

The Gunnison River began flowing along its current path approximately

Black Canyon of the Gunnison National Park

10 to 15 million years ago. At this time, the Colorado Plateau and Great Basin were rapidly uplifted, forcing the river to cut down into the earth's surface. Initially, it carved through relatively soft volcanic and sedimentary rocks. Then, approximately 2 million years ago, it encountered hard metamorphic rocks. The river carved through these rocks at a rate of about one inch every hundred years. The canyon walls adjacent to the river were left mostly intact due to their resistance to erosion. This created the enormous cliff faces seen today, including the 2,250-foot-high Painted Wall.

As the river carved deeper, it exposed rocks that had been buried underground for eons. Some of the oldest exposed rock in Colorado can be found in the Black Canyon, including Precambrian gneiss, which dates back nearly two billion years. Other prominent rocks in the canyon are schist, pegmatite, and quartz monzonite.

The uncompromising terrain along the Black Canyon has long impeded human settlement. Although Native Americans lived in the vicinity of the Black Canyon for over 10,000 years, there is no evidence that they ever inhabited its river bottom. However, the Ute Indians were familiar with the canyon and must have stood in awe of its depth and immensity.

The Spanish were the first European explorers to send expeditions near the Black Canyon. Juan Rivera passed through the area in 1765, and he was followed by Fathers Dominguez and Escalante in 1776. However, neither expedition came across the Black Canyon. Fur traders and trappers also passed through the region in the early 19th century but again did not leave a record of the canyon.

The first detailed account of the Black Canyon came in 1853 when Captain John W. Gunnison encountered the gorge while trying to find a route for a transcontinental railroad. Gunnison concluded that, with great effort, a railroad could be built through the canyon. However, he and his men surveyed only the tamer, upper reaches of the canyon.

Although the transcontinental railroad ultimately bypassed Colorado, interest in a railroad through the Black Canyon persisted. In 1881, the Denver and Rio Grande Railroad commissioned Byron Bryant to survey the canyon to see if a line could be built through it. After several months of arduous work, Bryant concluded that any attempt to construct a railroad through the entire length of the canyon would be nearly impossible.

The Denver and Rio Grande was able to construct a railroad through the first fifteen miles of the gorge, located in present-day Curecanti National Recreation Area. This track was laid at a cost of $165,000 per mile, and the first train made its way through the upper canyon in August of 1882.

The construction of this railroad coincided with the arrival of many new settlers in the Uncompahgre Valley, located west of the Black Canyon. Many of these settlers took up farming and sold crops to miners in the mountain towns. Water was sparse in the area, and in the 1890s, residents began to contemplate diverting water from the Gunnison River to the valley.

In 1900, John Pelton organized a group of men to explore the entire length of the river within the Black Canyon in hopes of discovering a suitable spot for a diversion tunnel. This group was ill-prepared for a journey through the formidable canyon. They abandoned their boat partway through and made a treacherous climb to the canyon rim.

Despite this failure, the idea of a diversion tunnel persisted. In 1901, Abraham Lincoln Fellows and Will Torrence made their own attempt to navigate the canyon. Instead of wooden boats, they floated down the river on air mattresses. With a lot of courage and a little luck, they made it safely through the entire length of the canyon.

The surveys done by Fellows and Torrence helped determine a suitable spot for a diversion tunnel. Construction began in earnest in 1905, and the Gunnison Tunnel was completed in 1909. This tunnel ran nearly six miles underground, making it the longest irrigation tunnel in the world at the time.

In the late 1920s, Reverend Mark Warner of Montrose became transfixed by the beauty of the Black Canyon. He, along with area civic groups, pushed for federal protection of the land. On March 2, 1933, Herbert Hoover signed a bill creating Black Canyon of the Gunnison National Monument. On October 21, 1999, Congress made the land a national park. The area below the rim of the canyon has been designated a national wilderness area.

The national park is home to a wide variety of plants and wildlife. Box elder, chokecherry, and cottonwood trees all grow along the canyon bottom, where the river provides ample amounts of water. Douglas firs and aspen trees cling tenaciously to existence along the dizzyingly steep slopes of the canyon. High atop the canyon rim are stands of pinyon pine, juniper, Gambel oak, and serviceberry.

Birds are among the few animals able to navigate into and out of the deep, inner reaches of the gorge. Species in the park include the golden eagle, turkey vulture, great horned owl, and peregrine falcon. The peregrine falcon was pushed to the brink of extinction in the 1970s, but it made a comeback and was removed from the endangered species list in 1999.

Larger mammals that are known to inhabit the park include mule deer, beavers, coyotes, bobcats, cougars, and black bears. Most mammals stay on top of the canyon rim or along the river bottom, but bighorn sheep will occasionally wander onto the craggy cliffs.

Today, approximately 400,000 visitors come to Black Canyon of the Gunnison National Park each year to gaze out over the immense canyon walls. The remote inner reaches of the canyon, however, remain nearly as inaccessible as they were when Captain Gunnison arrived in the region. Visitors can hike on trails to the canyon bottom, and kayakers can make their way down parts of the river, but the most rugged sections of the inner gorge seldom see the footsteps of man.

Above: Lichen-covered rocks rise high above the Gunnison River along the north rim.
p. 60: An eroded rock formation clings to the north rim at Kneeling Camel Overlook.

A cottonwood tree at the bottom of the canyon is ablaze with color in autumn.

Leaves on a yucca plant form remarkable, symmetrical patterns.

An aspen tree grows along a steep canyon hillside in early May.

The Milky Way rises above the Gunnison River and the Painted Wall in October.

Pulpit Rock Overlook provides a dizzying view of the Gunnison River 2,000 feet below.

Douglas firs grow at improbable spots along steep slopes of the canyon walls.

Jagged, eroded walls of the north rim are seen from a vantage point along the south rim.

Big sagebrush grows in a field atop the rim of the canyon.

Lichen grows in profusion on a rock face along the north rim.

Painted Wall View offers a stunning vista of the Gunnison River and Painted Wall.

A thin layer of fog rolls over the Black Canyon on a winter day.

Balanced Rock stands on the edge of the north rim of the Black Canyon.

At 2,250 feet high, Painted Wall is the highest cliff face in Colorado.

The tremendous amount of exposed rock creates ideal habitat for lichen.

The Gunnison River flows through majestic scenery near the eastern edge of the park.

A Douglas fir clings to existence atop the massive canyon walls.

Mesa Verde National Park in southwestern Colorado contains a remarkable array of architecture built by the Ancestral Puebloans approximately 1,000 years ago. It protects over 4,700 archaeological sites and 600 cliff dwellings.

The Ancestral Puebloans arrived in southwestern Colorado over 2,000 years ago and inhabited Mesa Verde from approximately 550 A.D. to 1300 A.D. The first settlers, called Basketmakers, relied primarily on farming for their sustenance. They developed some of the earliest irrigation systems in the region and were skilled at making pottery, baskets, and bow and ar-

MESA VERDE NATIONAL PARK

rows. They inhabited underground dwellings called pithouses, which were located on mesa tops and sometimes in cliff alcoves. Examples of some of these early structures can be found in the Badger House Community, located on Wetherill Mesa.

Around 750 A.D., the Native Americans in Mesa Verde began building basic houses aboveground. They gradually improved their architecture, and by 1000 A.D., they were using stone masonry to build structures as tall as three stories. During this time, the simple pithouses evolved into more elaborate underground structures known as kivas. Examples of these buildings and kivas can be seen today at the Far View dwellings, located near the visitor center.

In the 13th century, the Ancestral Puebloans moved from the mesa tops to protective alcoves along canyon walls. The reason for this move is not entirely understood, but it may have been for defensive purposes or for better protection from the elements. Although the Native Americans occupied these cliff alcoves for only one century, they left behind some of the most impressive structures ever built in Colorado.

The most famous of these structures is Cliff Palace. It is the largest cliff dwelling in North America and contained 160 rooms and 23 kivas. It housed around 100 people and was likely used for important ceremonies.

The second-largest cliff dwelling in Mesa Verde is Long House, which is located on Wetherill Mesa. This ruin had 150 rooms and 21 kivas. Near Long House is Step House, which contains reconstructed pit houses. This dwelling is unique in that there is

evidence that it was occupied during two different time periods, first around 600 A.D. and again around 1200 A.D. Other large cliff dwellings in the park are Spruce Tree House and Balcony House.

Around 1300 A.D., the Ancestral Puebloans mysteriously vanished from southwestern Colorado. The reason for their departure has puzzled archaeologists for decades. Some believe that invading tribes drove them from their homeland, but a more popular theory is that a long and persistent drought forced them to leave.

Subsequent tribes, such as the Ute Indians, knew about the stone structures built by the Ancestral Puebloans, but there is no evidence that these dwellings were ever inhabited after 1300 A.D.

The first U.S. citizen known to visit Mesa Verde was Dr. John S. Newberry, who was part of the San Juan Exploring Expedition. There is no account of him discovering ruins, but his expedition was the first to officially use the name Mesa Verde.

Following Newberry, miner John Moss spent many years exploring Mesa Verde's ruins, but he left no written description of his findings. Also, in 1884 a prospector named S.E. Osborn came across Balcony House and other smaller ruins. He would later describe what he saw in a newspaper article in 1886.

On December 18, 1888, Richard Wetherill and his brother-in-law Charlie Mason were searching for lost cattle when they spotted an enormous cliff dwelling that they named Cliff Palace. These two men became so fascinated by the ruins that they, and three of their brothers, spent the next eighteen years exploring the area for more archaeological sites. Although these cowboys were not formally trained, they gradually became skilled archaeologists. Richard Wetherill was also one of the earliest proponents of making Mesa Verde a national park.

In 1891, Swedish archaeologist Gustaf Nordenskiold came to Mesa Verde to explore and study the dwellings. He wrote a book called *The Cliff Dwellers of the Mesa Verde,* which gave the first detailed account of the ruins. Nordenskiold shipped many of the artifacts that he found back to Sweden. Officials in Durango attempted to stop him from taking these artifacts, but there was no law at the time to prevent him from doing so.

As word of the cliff dwellings in Mesa Verde spread, more and more visitors came to see these amazing structures. Many of them looted whatever items they could find and damaged the dwellings while camping inside of them. In response, a group of women formed the Colorado Cliff Dwellings Association, whose purpose was to preserve and protect the ancient ruins. They achieved their goal on June 29, 1906, when President Theodore Roosevelt created Mesa Verde National Park.

The creation of the national park not only protected the dwellings but also provided funds for excavation of the ruins. In 1908 and 1909, Dr. Jesse Walter Fewkes excavated and stabilized Spruce Tree House and Cliff Palace, both located on Chapin Mesa. In 1910, Jesse Nusbaum, who was one of the park's first superintendents, excavated Balcony House. Between 1958 and 1963, fifteen different

sites, including Long House, were excavated on Wetherill Mesa. In 1972, this part of the park was opened to visitors.

In addition to harboring ancient dwellings, Mesa Verde also shelters several rare plant and animal species. The peregrine falcon and Mexican spotted owl, both of which are threatened species, can be found in the park. Other uncommon animals living on the mesa are the black swallowtail butterfly, the Mesa Verde tiger beetle, and the Anasazi digger bee. Rare plants include the Cliff Palace milkvetch and Mesa Verde wandering aletes, both of which are found nowhere else on the planet.

In recent years, forest fires have threatened both the plants and dwellings in the park. Over 36,000 acres of land have burned since 1989, but the ruins escaped major harm. Following these fires, archaeologists did surveys to document and repair some of the damage. In the process, they discovered 682 new archaeological sites and found many new dams and irrigation systems built by the early inhabitants.

Today, approximately 600,000 people come to Mesa Verde National Park each year. Thanks to the efforts of those who have worked to preserve the land, visitors can get a glimpse of life in Colorado 1,000 years ago. Although the Ancestral Puebloans have long since departed, it is easy to picture their lives when coming face-to-face with their remarkable architecture. One can imagine early inhabitants farming along the mesa tops, tribal leaders performing a ceremony at Cliff Palace, or Native American children playing alongside the dwellings.

Above: Far View House is one of the largest mesa top sites, containing forty rooms.

p. 80: Cliff Palace is the largest and most famous cliff dwelling in North America.

Coyote Village is one of five villages among the Far View sites and contains five kivas.

Charred trees remain standing after forest fires burned over half of the park.

A beam of light shines into a restored kiva at Spruce Tree House.

A ladder emerges from a kiva in front of numerous rooms at Spruce Tree House.

Two large kivas are seen in front of the rooms of Balcony House.

At four stories high, Square Tower is the tallest cliff dwelling in the park.

Cliff Palace was constructed around 1200 A.D. and is the largest dwelling in the park.

A passageway inside Sun Temple is seen through a small window.

Late evening light illuminates Cedar Tree Tower, which was built around 1200 A.D.

A reconstructed pithouse can be seen in Step House on Wetherill Mesa.

Cliff Palace, which is located on Chapin Mesa, contained 23 kivas and 160 rooms.

Aptly-named Fire Temple lies below the charred remains of a forest fire.

New vegetation has sprung up since fires scorched Mesa Verde between 1989 and 2002.

Long House is the second largest cliff dwelling in Mesa Verde.

A large log juts out from an ancient ruin in Balcony House.

The cliff dwellings at Spruce Tree House are the third largest in the park.

Oak Tree House is located beneath the Mesa Top Loop Road on Chapin Mesa.

Mule deer, like this large buck, can be found throughout the park.

Although fires ravaged the trees in Mesa Verde, very little damage was done to the ruins.

Long before the Green and Yampa Rivers existed, a large ancient river flowed through what is now Dinosaur National Monument. This river was the source of water for countless animals, including turtles, crocodiles, and the largest of all land creatures, the dinosaur.

Around 150 million years ago, the landscape was stricken by a severe drought. As the ancient river dried up, the dinosaurs clung to existence at one of the few remaining watering holes, located where the Quarry Visitor Center in Utah is today. Once this watering hole evaporated, the dinosaurs succumbed to thirst and died.

DINOSAUR NATIONAL MONUMENT

When the drought finally ended, the river began to flow again, and it buried some of the dinosaur bones in the sand, where they became fossilized. They were subsequently covered by a layer of rock over one mile thick, which protected the fossils for millions of years. Over time, uplift and subsequent erosion of the landscape brought the dinosaur bones back near the surface.

The rocks in Dinosaur National Monument also hold the remains of a huge variety of other plants and animals, ranging from ancient sea creatures to petrified trees. These fossils help tell the story of how the environment and climate has evolved over time.

The oldest rock formations in the monument were deposited over one billion years ago when sediments eroded from an ancient mountain north of Dinosaur. These rocks, which are called the Uinta Mountain Group, can be observed today in the distinctive red walls of Canyon of Lodore in the northern part of the monument.

Over millions of years, vast amounts of sediment were deposited on top of the Uinta Mountain Group by seas, rivers, and wind. These sediments compacted into layers of rock nearly nine miles thick.

Beginning around 70 million years ago, continental plates pushed together, forming both the Rocky Mountains and a smaller range called the Uinta Mountains in northeastern Utah and northwestern Colorado. As these mountains were uplifted, rain, snow, and ice eroded some of the highest rock formations and deposited them in the lower valleys.

Approximately 6 million years ago, the Yampa River and Green River began flowing in their present courses. At first, they carved through the soft, young sediments deposited from the erosion of the Uintas. Then, during a period of renewed uplifting of the mountains, the rivers were forced to cut through harder, older rocks that are seen in the monument today.

The abundant supply of water provided by the rivers has attracted human inhabitants to this region for nearly 10,000 years. Artifacts such as spear points and grinding stones from the Paleo-Indians and Archaic people have been found within the monument.

Around 300 A.D., the Fremont Indians began growing corn, beans, and squash in fertile valleys along the rivers. The Fremont people also carved impressive artwork along boulders and cliff faces in the monument.

The first European explorers known to pass through the region were Fathers Dominguez and Escalante, who crossed over the Green River along the eastern edge of the monument during a Spanish expedition in 1776.

In the early 1800s, fur traders and trappers began traversing much of the western United States. In 1825, a group led by William H. Ashley took a boat down the Green River through Dinosaur National Monument in search of beaver pelts. They were probably the first people ever to float through these canyons. The famed mountain man Denis Julien also boated through the canyons in the 1830s.

John Wesley Powell led a more famous expedition down the Green River in 1869. The group smashed one of their boats in the monument in rapids that they later named Disaster Falls. However, Powell persevered, and his party became the first to float from Green River, Wyoming to the Grand Canyon in Arizona.

In the late 1800s, American settlers began colonizing most of Colorado. However, due to its remote location amidst steep, rugged canyons, Dinosaur National Monument attracted only a few, hardy residents. Amongst these people were the Mantles in Castle Park, the Chews in Pool Creek, and the Ruples in Island Park.

The first person to discover dinosaur bones in the monument was Earl Douglass, who unearthed the tail bones of an Apatosaurus on August 17, 1909. In subsequent years, an enormous number of additional specimens were discovered in the same quarry. Archaeologists shipped 350 tons of fossils from 9 different dinosaur species to the Carnegie Museum and other sites around the country.

Carnegie officials wanted to protect this valuable quarry and lobbied for federal protection of the fossils. They got their wish in 1915 when 80 acres were set aside by Woodrow Wilson as a national monument. Over 200,000 acres of land were added to the monument in 1938 to protect the spectacular canyons of the Green and Yampa Rivers.

Although these canyons received national monument status, they were not fully protected from development. In 1950, the U.S. Bureau of Reclamation proposed building two large dams within Dinosaur National Monument. One dam would have been constructed at Echo Park, just past the confluence of the Green and Yampa Rivers. The other would have been built in Split Mountain Gorge in Utah. Conservation groups strongly protested the construction of these dams, since they believed national parks and monuments should be protected from such development. Their efforts ultimately paid off, and Congress did not approve the construction of dams within the monument.

Although the dam projects were canceled, the ecosystem has still been impacted by human activities, including trapping and trading, the introduction of livestock, fire suppression, and the construction of a dam upstream at Flaming Gorge. As a result, four fishes that are endemic to the region are currently endangered, and bison, grizzly bears, and bighorn sheep were eliminated from the national monument.

Man's ability to damage the landscape also comes with an ability to repair some of this damage. Bighorn sheep were reintroduced in 1952, and they now thrive along the steep canyon walls. Also, the peregrine falcon was driven to the brink of extinction in the 1970s, but it has made a remarkable comeback and can now be seen soaring high above the monument. Three of the endangered fish species also find sanctuary in the Yampa River, which is the last free-flowing river in the Colorado River system.

The irreparable harm that would have been caused by dams in the monument can serve as a reminder that sometimes nature is best left alone. President Theodore Roosevelt summed up this sentiment well when he said during a speech at the Grand Canyon in 1903, "Leave it as it is. You cannot improve on it. The ages have been at work on it, and man can only mar it."

Above: A log juts into the Yampa River on the eastern side of the park.
p. 104: Steamboat Rock is reflected in the Green River near Echo Park.

Dramatic scenery abounds near the confluence of the Green and Yampa Rivers.

The Green River cuts through one-billion-year-old rocks in Canyon of Lodore.

A small tree clings to existence on a canyon wall above Warmsprings rapids.

The twists and turns of the Yampa River are seen from Harding Hole Overlook.

Streaks of desert varnish rise above a pair of pine trees along the Yampa River.

Signature Cave overlooks the Yampa River near Harding Hole.

A large petroglyph depicting a bighorn is etched along a cliff face in Echo Park.

Lush vegetation grows along the Green River in Lodore Canyon.

Black desert varnish offers dramatic contrast to the red canyon walls.

Streaks of desert varnish on Tiger Wall rise high above the Yampa River.

Steamboat Rock is reflected in the Green River at Echo Park.

The Gates of Lodore is reflected in the Green River at sunrise.

The Green River flows past Cottonwood Trees that were charred by a forest fire.

Golden light shines through the opening to Whispering Cave in late afternoon.

The last light of day illuminates Harpers Corner above the Green River.

Colorado National Monument in western Colorado harbors some of the most ruggedly beautiful scenery in the state. The land rises high above the Grand Valley and contains an intricate network of canyons, cliffs, and sandstone rock formations.

The rock formations in the monument were created through a complex series of geologic events occurring over an immense period of time. Beginning around 300 million years ago, the Uncompahgre Plateau was thrust upward over 10,000 feet by tectonic forces. Over time, this plateau gradually eroded back down to elevations near sea level. As it did so, the cli-

COLORADO NATIONAL MONUMENT

mate became drier, and the plateau was periodically covered with sand dunes, which eventually compacted into sandstone.

The Uncompahgre Plateau was uplifted again during the creation of the Rocky Mountains, beginning around 70 million years ago. Today, this plateau is approximately 100 miles long and 25 miles wide. Colorado National Monument is located at the far northern end of the uplift.

As water from melting snow and summer rain flowed from the high mesas of the Uncompahgre Plateau down to the Colorado River, it carved out several impressive canyons in Colorado National Monument. The rocks were further eroded when water seeped into cracks, froze and expanded. Other erosive forces that have shaped the landscape include wind and even plant growth.

In Colorado National Monument, Kayenta Sandstone located high atop the canyon rims is harder than the shaly sandstone beneath it. This has prevented the upper layers of sandstone from eroding as quickly as those beneath and has formed enormous sandstone monoliths rising as high as 550 feet.

The first humans to witness these spectacular pinnacles were undoubtedly the Native Americans. They inhabited the Grand Valley below the monument for thousands of years, but there is no evidence that they ever lived within the lands encompassing Colorado National Monument.

The Ancestral Puebloans, who constructed many cliff dwellings to the south, began planting crops along the Colorado River in the Grand Valley almost 1,700 years ago. They were later supplanted by the Ute Indians, who arrived in Colorado around 1300 A.D. The Utes inhabited this landscape until 1881 when they were driven onto reservations in Utah.

The first Europeans known to pass through the Grand Valley were Fathers Francisco Dominguez and Silvestre Velez de Escalante, during a Spanish expedition in 1776. Fur trappers and traders arrived in the region in the early 1880s, and in 1839 Joseph Roubdeau established a fur trading post near present-day Grand Junction.

On September 7, 1881, O.D. Russell and William McGinley established the first ranch in the Grand Valley. George A. Crawford built a house there the following month, and on October 10, 1881, he helped found the town of Grand Junction. Just one year later, the Denver and Rio Grande Railroad arrived in town.

In 1906, John Otto came to Grand Junction and fell in love with an obscure landscape to the south that is now Colorado National Monument. Otto single-handedly built several foot trails over the rugged terrain and named many of the geologic formations. On July 4, 1910, Otto made a daring ascent of Independence Monument and placed the American flag at its summit.

Otto campaigned hard for the land to be protected as a national park. Although it never reached this status, President William Taft created Colorado National Monument on May 24, 1911. Otto was hired as the first park ranger, a position he held until 1927.

Early on, the mesas in Colorado National Monument were difficult to access, as there were only hiking trails in the monument. Between 1912 and 1921, a footpath called Trail of the Serpent was expanded to a wagon road using only private money and county funds. However, this road was very steep and treacherous and was often referred to as "the most dangerous road ever built."

In 1933, the Civilian Conservation Corps began work on a better road through the monument, called Rim Rock Drive. Construction of this road was interrupted in 1942 because of World War II. Work continued in 1949, and the road was finally completed in 1950. The CCC also installed water and telephone lines, developed a picnic area, and constructed a ranger's residence.

In 1949, a movie called Devil's Doorway was filmed in Colorado National Monument. Although it was not commercially successful, this was a groundbreaking film, as it was the first to depict Native Americans in a positive light. The movie American Flyers was also shot in the monument in 1985.

Since Colorado National Monument has been protected by the federal government for nearly a century, it provides thousands of acres of pristine natural habitat for plant and wildlife species. The desert environment is ideal for reptiles, including lizards, bull snakes, and the occasional midget faded rattlesnake. The cliffs provide shelter for many birds, including falcons, turkey vultures, bald eagles, and red-tailed hawks.

Among the mammals in the park are mule deer, elk, coyotes, foxes, bobcats, desert bighorns, and mountain lions. At one time, a herd of bison also roamed through the monument. These animals were introduced by John Otto in 1926, as part of a wildlife preserve. The bison were removed from the park in 1983, due to overgrazing of the canyon floors.

Millions of years ago, much larger animals roamed this land. In 1900, Dr. Elmer Riggs found the bones of a Brachiosaurus just outside the boundaries of the monument on what became known as Riggs Hill. This was the first dinosaur of its kind ever discovered, and at the time it was the largest dinosaur ever unearthed. In subsequent years, numerous other dinosaur fossils have been found near the monument.

Today, approximately 400,000 people visit Colorado National Monument each year. Those who come can thank John Otto for the tireless work he put into making the land accessible to the public and preserving it for future generations. Most of the trails that Otto built are still in use today, and many of the rock formations bear names that Otto gave them a century ago.

Above: Virga produced by a storm cloud hovers over the distant Book Cliffs.
p. 124: Snow covers Monument Canyon beneath Kissing Couple and Praying Hands.

A gnarled juniper tree atop Wedding Canyon frames distant sandstone pillars.

Massive rock formations, including Pipe Organ and Kissing Couple, are lit by the setting sun.

Dramatic clouds float above a dead pinyon pine along Canyon Rim Trail.

Numerous icicles formed on a cliff face near the northern edge of the monument.

The Coke Ovens bathe in late evening light beneath picturesque cloud formations.

Window Rock Trail provides dramatic views of Wedding Canyon and Monument Canyon.

Grand View offers a stunning vista of Monument Canyon beneath a building thunderhead.

A large monolith known as Pipe Organ is seen from the end of Otto's Trail.

A raven stands on a gnarled pinyon pine located atop Wedding Canyon.

The setting sun illuminates rock formations in Monument Canyon.

Balanced Rock stands above pinyon pines on a foggy winter day.

Rock formations at Devil's Kitchen rise above a snow-covered landscape.

Canyons of the Ancients was created in 2000 and is one of Colorado's newest national monuments. It comprises 164,000 acres and contains over 6,000 archaeological sites. In stark contrast to the more famous ruins at Mesa Verde, most of the sites here are unpublicized and see very few visitors each year.

Some of the earliest ruins found in Canyons of the Ancients were built by Ancestral Puebloan people known as Basketmakers. They arrived in the area around 1500 B.C. and initially relied on hunting and gathering to procure food. Over time, they

CANYONS OF THE ANCIENTS NATIONAL MONUMENT

became skilled farmers and developed complex irrigation systems throughout the region.

Initially, the Ancestral Puebloans inhabited underground pithouses. Around 750 A.D., they began building houses aboveground using poles and mud. By 1000 A.D., they had started making houses using stone masonry and were able to construct much larger, sturdier buildings.

One of the most impressive structures built with stone masonry is called Lowry Pueblo. It was constructed around 1060 A.D. and contained 40 rooms and several kivas, including a great kiva. The great kiva may have been used for large gatherings and ceremonies involving neighboring communities.

Another notable village is Escalante Pueblo, which is located on a hill above the visitor center. It contained approximately 28 rooms that were built around a kiva and was occupied between 1100 A.D. and 1200 A.D.

A much larger village, called Sand Canyon Pueblo, is located 15 miles west of Escalante Pueblo. This pueblo had approximately 420 rooms and 100 kivas, making it one of the largest and most important villages in the region. It is believed to have been built around 1250 A.D. and inhabited for only 30 years. Although the village was partially excavated between 1983 and 1993, it was backfilled and is now buried entirely underground.

The Ancestral Puebloans also built numerous tall, round structures known as towers. One tower that remains standing is located at Painted Hand Pueblo. There are pictographs of hands painted on a boulder beneath this tower.

Around 1200 A.D., the Ancestral Puebloans began building many of their structures in cliff alcoves rather than mesa tops. Several small cliff dwellings can be seen today along Sand Canyon Trail.

After the Ancestral Puebloans departed their homeland around 1300 A.D., they were replaced in the Four Corners region by Ute and Navajo Indians. Archaeologists have discovered hogans, brush shelters, wickiups, and petroglyphs made by these tribes within the monument.

The first European explorers to enter the region around Canyons of the Ancients were the Spanish, who came in search of travel routes to California. In 1776, Fathers Francisco Dominguez and Silvestre Velez de Escalante came across the ancient ruins that are now named Dominguez Pueblo and Escalante Pueblo.

American settlers began colonizing the land in southwestern Colorado in the late 1880s. Like the Ancestral Puebloans before them, these pioneers established farms throughout the area. Many of the farms and ranches have remained occupied by the same family until the present day.

Today, large expanses of rolling farmland are interspersed with primordial landscapes that harbor ancient treasures. Although some of these artifacts are housed at the visitor center, many more remain buried at the same spots where the Native Americans abandoned them nearly 1,000 years ago.

Above: Two impressive stone towers stand in a remote canyon.
p. 142: Clouds hover above an ancient ruin at Painted Hand Pueblo.

Paintbrush and yucca plants thrive in many parts of the park.

A large cliff dwelling stands in a remote canyon in Canyons of the Ancients.

A small ruin sits hidden beneath an alcove in the Sand Canyon area.

A well-preserved ruin along Sand Canyon Trail offers a good view of Sleeping Ute Mountain.

An impressive dwelling was constructed in a deep alcove in the Sand Canyon area.

Several Ancestral Puebloan ruins stand in a cliff dwelling along Sand Canyon Trail.

Two ancient structures remain standing along a cliff face in Sand Canyon.

The late evening sun illuminates a great kiva at Lowry Pueblo.

A secluded ruin is lit by the setting sun, as the full moon rises over Sleeping Ute Mountain.

A small doorway leads into the large and well-preserved Lowry Pueblo.

Escalante Pueblo sits atop a hillside above the Anasazi Heritage Center.

The rising sun illuminates a small door and windows at Lowry Pueblo.

The first light of day reflects off a rock wall adjacent to Saddle Horn Ruin in Sand Canyon.

A petroglyph panel was carved on a rock face near the Utah border.

Dramatic storm clouds float over Canyons of the Ancients on a summer evening.

Hovenweep National Monument protects several ancient Native American villages in Colorado and Utah. These villages were inhabited by Ancestral Puebloans, who built an enormous number of stone buildings throughout the Four Corners area. Although they inhabited this region for hundreds of years, most of the structures at Hovenweep were constructed between 1200 A.D. and 1300 A.D.

The village with the most intact ruins in Hovenweep is called Square Tower Group and lies in Utah. It has 30 kivas and several towers. The other site in Utah is called Cajon Group, which contains the remains of a small

HOVENWEEP
NATIONAL MONUMENT

village and some pictographs.

The easternmost site in Colorado is known as Holly Group. It is located along the rim of Keeley Canyon and contains structures known as Boulder House and Tilted Tower. Boulder House is perched precariously atop a large boulder, and it is a testament to the skill of the builders that it remains standing today. Tilted Tower got its name because the rock on which it was built shifted sometime after the structure was abandoned. The top of the tower collapsed, and only a small part of the lower section remains standing today.

Archaeologists are unsure of the exact purposes that the towers served. They may have been used as celestial observatories, defensive structures, storage facilities, or houses. They were often built near springs and seeps, which provided water and had religious significance to the early inhabitants.

A short distance to the northeast of Holly Group is Horseshoe Group. Horseshoe Tower is the most prominent ruin at this location. It stands atop Horseshoe Canyon and may have been built for defensive purposes. Horseshoe House, which is made up of four structures arranged in the shape of a horseshoe, is also part of this group of ruins.

Hackberry Group is located just east of the Horseshoe ruins. It may have had the largest population of any of the sites in Colorado since Hackberry Canyon had an abundant supply of water.

Several miles to the northeast of Hackberry stands Cutthroat Castle. This village is unique in Hovenweep in that its structures were not built at the head of a canyon but further downstream. It contains one of the few kivas that was constructed aboveground.

The easternmost site in Hovenweep National Monument is Goodman Point. In 1889, this unit became the first archaeological site in the United States to be protected by the federal government. It is one of the largest sites in Hovenweep, containing architecture ranging in size from small villages to large communities. This site is believed to have had a limited population from 200 to 450 A.D. and likely had many more residents from 900 to 1300 A.D. The structures here are of more interest to archaeologists than to tourists, as they are mostly collapsed and partially buried.

The first U.S. resident to see the ruins at Hovenweep was W.D. Huntington, who wrote about them during a Mormon expedition across Utah in 1854. The land was given its name, meaning "desert valley" in the Ute language, by pioneer photographer William Henry Jackson, who photographed Square Tower Group in 1874. J.W. Fewkes, who surveyed the area for the Smithsonian Institution from 1917 to 1918, pushed for protection of the land by the federal government. His efforts paid off when President Warren Harding created Hovenweep National Monument on March 2, 1923.

Although the structures at Hovenweep were set aside as a national monument nearly a century ago, they remain relatively unknown, since they are tucked away in a remote part of the Colorado Plateau. Those who visit the ruins can immerse themselves in a primordial landscape that has remained mostly unchanged since the Ancestral Puebloans inhabited the area in ages past.

Horseshoe Tower stands high atop Horseshoe Canyon in far western Colorado.

Above: Intricate patterns of rock and mud form the wall of a ruin in Cutthroat Castle.
p. 160: Boulder House in Holly Group stands beneath a canopy of stars.

Ancient ruins dot the landscape along Hackberry Canyon.

A small tower is seen from atop a larger ruin at Cutthroat Castle.

Horseshoe House is composed of four rooms in the shape of a horseshoe.

Black, hardened cryptobiotic soil fosters the growth of many plants in the monument.

Yucca House National Monument lies at the base of Sleeping Ute Mountain in southwestern Colorado. It is 34 acres in size and receives fewer than 1,000 visitors per year, making it the smallest and least-visited national monument in Colorado. There are no signs leading visitors to the area, and Yucca House itself is buried underground.

Although this monument may appear unimpressive at first glance, it hides one of the largest and most significant Ancestral Puebloan ruins in Colorado. Archaeologists believe that the Ancestral Puebloans occupied this dwelling from 1150 to 1300 A.D. It likely

Yucca House National Monument

served as an important community center for Native Americans and may also have been a trade center.

There are two large mounds of dirt in Yucca House that cover the once-spectacular structures. The larger mound is known as the West Complex, or Upper House. It had approximately 600 rooms and at least 100 kivas. The smaller mound is known as the Lower House. It contains the only wall that is presently visible in the monument and had at least eight rooms, with a great kiva at its center.

A spring flows through Yucca House, creating some marshland and making the area suitable for farming. The Ancestral Puebloans developed sophisticated techniques to grow their crops and constructed ditches and reservoirs to carry and store water. Some of their most important crops were beans, corn, and squash.

The first documentation of Yucca House by the United States was made by Professor William Holmes during the U.S. Geological Survey in 1877. At the time, Yucca House was the largest Ancestral Puebloan dwelling discovered in the southwestern United States. Holmes thought that the structure had been built by the Aztecs and thus named the area Aztec Springs. This name was later changed to Yucca House, due to the large amounts of yucca growing on nearby Sleeping Ute Mountain.

The first owner of the land containing Yucca House was a man named Henry Van Kleek. On July 2, 1919, Van Kleek donated 9.6 acres of this land, including all of Yucca House, to the federal government, hoping that the ruins would be excavated. On December 19, 1919, Woodrow Wilson established Yucca House as a national monument.

Despite Van Kleek's wishes, archaeologists have chosen not to excavate Yucca House. They fear that the ruins could be damaged when exposed to the erosive forces of Mother Nature or to vandals or careless visitors. They also want to keep some ruins buried so that future archaeologists may be able to glean more information from the site with improved excavation methods and better scientific equipment.

There has been a limited amount of work and scientific studies undertaken at Yucca House. In 1964, Al Lancaster stabilized the one visible wall in the monument. Later that year, Al Schroeder discovered that some of the walls in the monument were constructed of adobe, which was unusual for inhabitants in this region.

Another person who contributed to the preservation and understanding of Yucca House was Hallie Ismay, who owned land near the ruins from 1921 to 2002. In the late 1990s, she donated 24 acres to the monument, which allowed for the protection of nearby sites. It also provided an opportunity for more non-invasive research, including a study done in 2000 to remap the ruins using current scientific methods.

As it has for the past 700 years, Yucca House today remains a quiet and peaceful landscape. A coyote or bobcat will occasionally wander amidst the ruins as a solitary hawk flies high above searching for mice and voles. Every so often, a visitor will make their way to this remote national monument to marvel at what little remains visible of a once-mighty community.

Above: A Claret Cup cactus grows in Yucca House.
p. 168: Only one portion of a wall remains unburied within the monument.

The rising sun illuminates Sleeping Ute Mountain and the one exposed wall at the Lower House.

High atop a mesa near a towering monolith called Chimney Rock sits one of the most captivating archaeological sites in Colorado. This site is known as the Great House Pueblo and was built by the Chacoans around 1093 A.D.

The Chacoans were Ancestral Puebloans who resided mainly in northwestern New Mexico. Their territory stretched into present-day Colorado, and the ruins at Chimney Rock represent the northernmost portion of their land.

The Great House Pueblo may have been built below Chimney Rock to observe and celebrate the Major Lunar Standstill. This event occurs every 18.6 years when the moon rises at its northernmost point in the sky. As viewed from the Great House, it

CHIMNEY ROCK
NATIONAL MONUMENT

rises directly between the pillars of Chimney Rock and Companion Rock. To commemorate this event, Chacoans from many neighboring communities may have gathered together for festivals and ceremonies at the Great House.

Astronomer priests likely made other astronomical observations at structures near Chimney Rock. A precise understanding of celestial patterns and events was important for religious ceremonies and for planting and harvesting crops. They may have shared this information with tribes to the south using a signal fire near the Great House. This fire would have been visible to observers on Huerfano Peak, who, in turn, would have been able to signal inhabitants of Chaco Canyon.

Although the Great House Pueblo is the best-known site in the region, it is just one of approximately 200 archaeological sites located in Chimney Rock National Monument. Most of these sites have not yet been excavated, or have been backfilled, and are buried underground. The four excavated sites that can be seen today are the Great House Pueblo, Great Kiva, Ridge House, and Pit House. Like the Great House Pueblo, the Great Kiva was probably used for community gatherings and ceremonies. Ridge House and Pit House are examples of family dwellings that were common throughout the area. The oldest family dwelling discovered at Chimney Rock is called the Salvage Site and dates back to 925 A.D. This ruin is now mostly backfilled.

At its peak, Chimney Rock was divided into eight distinct villages that housed around 2,000 people. The inhabitants relied mostly on farming to procure food. They likely traded important resources, including agricultural products, timber, and game animals, with other Chacoan communities over long distances.

Around 1125 A.D., barely 30 years after the construction of the Great House, a drought is believed to have afflicted much of the Chacoan culture. The lack of water, combined with an overuse of resources, appears to have forced residents to abandon Chimney Rock sometime between 1125 to 1130 A.D. It's possible that diseases and epidemics also contributed to the community's demise. This abandonment came much earlier than other nearby Ancestral Puebloan sites, like Mesa Verde, which were inhabited until around 1300 A.D. The exact combination of events that led to this exodus may never be known.

After its abandonment, the structures slowly began to crumble, and sedimentary deposits built up over what remained of them. Eventually, this once-great community was buried almost entirely underground.

The earliest attempt to excavate these ruins was made by Jean Allard Jeancon in the 1920s. However, the structures were not stabilized, which led to a rapid deterioration of the sites. Some of the ruins had to be backfilled to prevent further degradation.

In the early 1970s, the Forest Service excavated and restored additional sites, including the Great House Pueblo, using more advanced techniques. Some work has been done since then to stabilize the ruins.

Due to the wealth of archaeological sites surrounding Chimney Rock, President Barack Obama established Chimney Rock National Monument on September 21, 2012. Today, visitors can take guided tours to this remarkable land that time forgot. Most visitors will make the short but steep hike to the Great House Pueblo. If they are able to visit during the next Major Lunar Standstill, they can witness the same phenomenon that inspired the Chacoans nearly 1,000 years earlier. As the sun sets over the western horizon, the full moon will repeat its eternal dance with Earth and once again rise between the imposing pillars of Chimney Rock and Companion Rock.

Above: Ridge House is one of four excavated sites at Chimney Rock.
p. 174: The Great House Pueblo, which was built 900 years ago, lies beneath Chimney Rock.

The last light of day illuminates the stone structures at Great House Pueblo.

Browns Canyon National Monument encompasses 21,586 acres and provides spectacular views of the towering peaks of the Sawatch Range. There are few roads within the monument, so the best way to see it is by hiking or rafting. The majority of visitors choose the latter, as the Arkansas River offers some of the best white water rafting in the nation.

While floating down the river, rafters can gaze in wonder at the 1.6 billion-year-old granodiorite rock that rises abruptly from the river's edge. If they are lucky, they may be able to view some of the diverse wildlife that inhabits the monument. Some of the larger mammals found here include bighorn sheep, elk, black bears, mountain lions, bobcats, and coyotes.

BROWNS CANYON NATIONAL MONUMENT

The Arkansas River also attracts many fishermen to its banks, since it has abundant populations of brown and rainbow trout.

Visitors to this land may get the impression that the jagged rocks and massive peaks have been around since time immemorial. However, fossils found inside the monument tell a much different story. Archaeologists have unearthed fossils of invertebrates, bony fish, and sharks that lived along an ocean reef in this region over 300 million years ago.

Subsequent uplift of the land resulted in the creation of the Ancestral Rocky Mountains. This mountain range eventually eroded back down, and the land again became covered by a sea over 100 million years ago. This sea was inhabited by extraordinary creatures, including the enormous Mosasaur with alligator-like jaws and the huge, long-necked Elasmasaurus.

The ancient sea gave way to the Rocky Mountains around 70 million years ago, as continental plates pushed the land ever higher. As the mountains rose, rivers and streams began surging down the peaks, creating many broad valleys. The Arkansas River valley was one of the last valleys to be formed below the Sawatch Range. It has existed for less than 30 million years.

Some of the more remarkable scenery within this valley was sculpted during a series of glacial periods beginning around 2.6 million years ago. As colossal glaciers gradually moved across the landscape, they carved cirques, terraces, and moraines that can be seen within the monument today.

Near the end of the most recent glacial period, Native Americans began migrating across much of North America. Archaeological sites within Browns Canyon suggest that Paleo-Indians first entered the monument as far back as 13,000 years ago. They were likely drawn to the Arkansas River Valley because of its ample supply of fresh water and bountiful wildlife populations.

In later years, many different tribes resided in the area, including the Ute and Jicarilla Apaches. The first American explorer to pass through the valley was Zebulon Pike during his expedition to Colorado in 1806-1807. Not long afterward, many fur trappers and traders came to the Arkansas River in search of animal pelts.

In the late 1870s, an enormous rush of prospectors headed to Leadville and neighboring communities in search of silver. Although little silver was ever discovered in Browns Canyon, it did become an important area for fluorite mining. Fluorite is a colorful mineral that has many industrial and ornamental uses.

In recent times, as Browns Canyon became known for its cultural artifacts, biological diversity, and recreational opportunities, area residents began calling for greater protection of the land. This call was answered when President Barack Obama created Browns Canyon National Monument on Feb.19, 2015.

Today, visitors can get lost within a landscape that has changed little since man first set foot in Colorado. From an elevation of 7,400 feet at the river's edge, hikers can climb to elevations exceeding 10,000 feet. From high atop rocky crags, they can find astounding views of the Sawatch Range, with the ribbon-like waters of the Arkansas River visible far below.

This river, and others like it, are gradually but persistently carrying sediments from the mountains down toward sea level. In the far distant future, this erosion will cause the Rocky Mountains to shrink and eventually disappear. Perhaps the land will again become covered by a shallow sea inhabited by creatures that we cannot begin to imagine today.

Above: A colorful sunset lights up the sky over Browns Canyon.
p. 180: The Arkansas River flows through rock outcrops below the Sawatch Range.

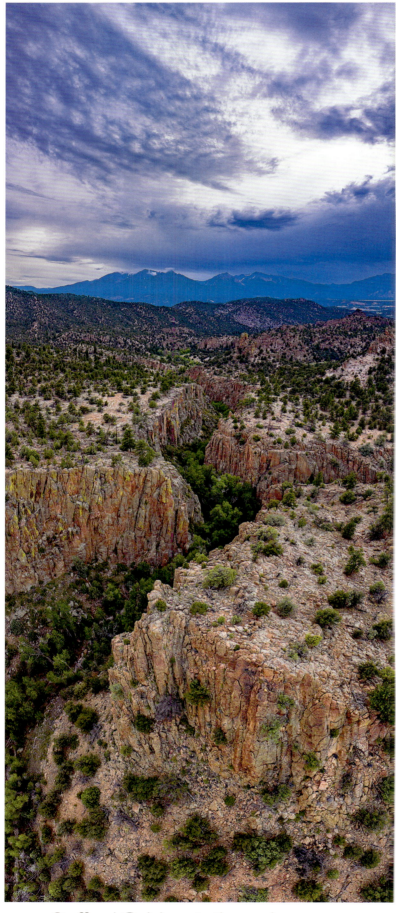

Stafford Gulch cuts through an area known as The Reef below Mount Shavano and Mount Antero.

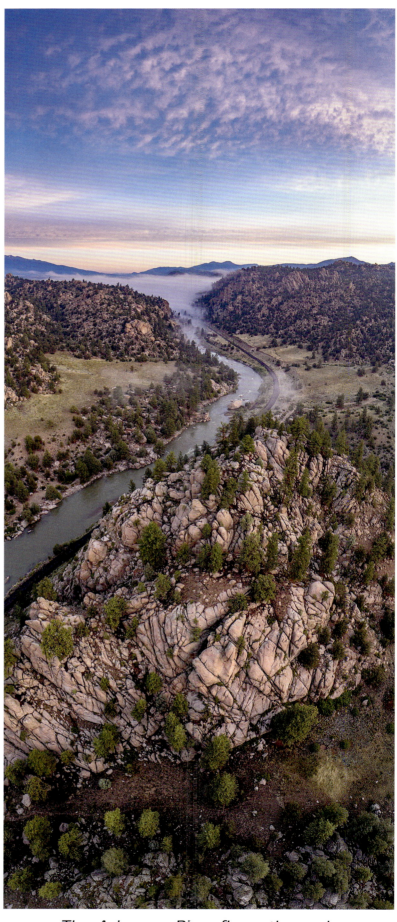

The Arkansas River flows through picturesque rock formations at sunrise in Browns Canyon.

Low-lying clouds hover above Browns Canyon National Monument at sunrise.

Florissant Fossil Beds National Monument provides a hint of what life was like in Colorado 34 million years ago. In this distant epoch, massive volcanoes erupted throughout the state, spewing lava across the landscape. One particularly violent eruption occurred near Florissant Valley and periodically covered the area with volcanic ash, pumice, mud, and clay. This debris buried and preserved large amounts of animal and plant life that inhabited the region at the time.

Over 1,700 species of fossilized animals and petrified plants have been discovered in Florissant Fossil Beds. The vast majority of these fossils are from small plants and invertebrates, but there are also larger fossils from fish, birds, and mammals. The biggest and most impressive fossils are the petrified stumps of giant Sequoia

Florissant Fossil Beds National Monument

trees. These are amongst the largest petrified trees in the world, and they offer a glimpse of the colossal redwood forests that grew in Colorado when the Rocky Mountains were half their current age.

The first people to lay eyes on the petrified Sequoia trees may have been the Paleo-Indians, who entered Colorado over 10,000 years ago. Archaeologists have discovered tools made by these prehistoric inhabitants near Florissant Fossil Beds that date back nearly 8,000 years. They have also found evidence that the Archaic people, who succeeded the Paleo-Indians in Colorado, inhabited this region.

Around 1300 A.D., the Ute Indians arrived in Colorado. They were a nomadic people, and their homeland included much of Colorado's Rocky Mountains, including Florissant Fossil Beds. Florissant Valley also lay close to the terrain inhabited by the plains tribes, and these Native Americans may have also visited the fossil beds.

The first American settler in Florissant Valley was Judge James Castello. He arrived in 1870 and constructed a house and hotel in a new town that he called Florissant. Castello later built a trading post, a general store, and a post office in town.

The first settlement within the boundaries of Florissant Fossil Beds National Monument was made by David P. Long, who arrived in 1873. Long built a house and a school on his property, and he was also a preacher for the community.

In 1874, geologist Arthur C. Peal came to the fossil beds as part of the Hayden Expedition. He was the first to write about the scientific value of the area. Many other scientists would later come to study the incredible array of fossil life in the valley.

In 1878, Adeline Hornbek migrated to Florissant, where she built a log house. Hornbek was a single parent who served on the school board and worked at James Castello's general store. Her homestead has been preserved and is now one of the primary attractions at Florissant Fossil Beds.

As more people traveled to the area, word of the remarkable fossils and petrified trees spread. In the 1880s, a commercial quarry was established, and many of the fossils were sold to visitors. Entire petrified trees were relocated, and the trunks of the largest Sequoias were spared only because of the difficulty in removing them.

Two more commercial enterprises that permitted visitors to collect fossils were established at Florissant Fossil Beds in the 1920s. One was located near the Big Stump and contained a fossil exhibit at a ranch called Colorado Petrified Forest. The other was called Pike Petrified Forest, where visitors came to view a grouping of three petrified Sequoia trees known as the Redwood Trio. The visitor center and ticket booth that was used at Pike Petrified Forest is still used as the visitor center for the national monument today.

Although the National Park Service was aware of the need to protect the fossil beds from commercial activity for many decades, members of the government were slow to take action. They were forced to act in 1969 when developers prepared to build a housing complex in Florissant Valley. Estella Leopold formed a citizens' group called The Defenders of Florissant, and they obtained a restraining order to stop construction. On August 20, 1969, President Richard Nixon signed a bill establishing Florissant Fossil Beds as a national monument.

Despite some of the early vandalism, Florissant Fossil Beds remains an impressive sight today. The visitor center contains fossils of life that inhabited Colorado 34 million years ago, and the monument itself has numerous petrified Sequoia trees that draw approximately 70,000 visitors each year. These ancient behemoths, which were part of a species that is now extinct, remind us of the constant evolution of life that has occurred in the past and that will continue into the indefinite future.

The Hornbek Homestead was built in 1878 by Adeline Hornbek.

Above: The Redwood Trio is the only known trio of petrified redwoods in the world.
p. 186: The Big Stump is the largest unburied petrified Sequoia in the monument.

The remnants of a once-immense Sequoia tree stand west of the Redwood Trio.

A petrified Sequoia tree stump lies just outside the visitor center.

Wildflowers grow atop the fossilized stump of an ancient Sequoia tree.

A pair of picturesque windows is seen on the side of the house at Hornbek Homestead.